The ARTIST and the CROW

The ARTIST and the CROW

by Dan Stryk

PURDUE UNIVERSITY PRESS
West Lafayette, Indiana

Published 1984

Library of Congress Cataloging in Publication Data

Stryk, Dan, 1951–
    The artist and the crow.

    I. Title.
PS3569.T75A88 1984   811'.54   84-11551
ISBN 0-911198-71-7

Printed in the United States of America

For Suzanne and Theo

CONTENTS

SCENES FROM A TRAGICOMEDY

OF BLIGHT AND FAITH

ACKNOWLEDGMENTS

Grateful acknowledgment is made to the following publications in which some of these poems first appeared: *Ararat, The Beloit Poetry Journal, The Chariton Review, Confrontation, Crosscurrents, The Hollins Critic, Kansas Quarterly, Kayak, Midstream, The Missouri Review, New Mexico Humanities Review, Poem, Poetry Now, Southern Humanities Review, Southern Poetry Review, Sou'wester,* and *Western Humanities Review.*

"Swelter" (as a single poem) was anthologized in *Writers Forum 6,* University of Colorado, 1980 (distributed by Swallow Press).

A few of these poems, in earlier forms, first appeared in the limited-edition chapbook *To Make a Life,* Confluence Press (Lewis-Clark State College, Lewiston, Idaho, 1980).

I am grateful to the National Endowment for the Arts for a 1982 Creative Writing Fellowship, during which most of these poems were written or begun.

. . . ., humped back,
bird on pole—eyes, warm
as folded wings, reflect
the penumbra of the universe.

● ● ● ● ● ●

Birth's a crack in the
ground plan. Since universe
is no bigger than its head,
where's the bird to fly?

● ● ● ● ●

—*Shinkichi Takahashi*

Cornlands

for Art Dellabella

ILLINOIS TOWNS

DeKalb

Summer:

fat winged fields
sway russet-tipped, town's
eclipsed past

June. North, south
silos loom
barbed flats, flare

into blue heat.
Slow Greek taverns
stud the shop-line, east...

Winter

ribs the bluelit pane
of Leon's Tap,
a lucent shell coats barbs...

•

Steel hollow sun
floats high out toward Chicago.
Below,

the yellow spoor
of some lame
cur

kindles the snow...

Carbondale

Terminal:

Through high-noon torpor
of a small freight town,
the whistle's blare,

like a memory, rattles in dry air,
among the serried clapboards,
ragged blacktop ways.

Parched: the dull plant files
of tomato, pumpkin, squash
cling to their crude trellises

against the roughboard
walls, like old soldiers
to their walkers. Within,

clamped tight and dusty-grey,
shutters frame an image
of the crippled drunk, hobbling

round the terminal,
scolding benches
flocked with muttering age—

Then, leering at his famous watch,
stiffens up
to hail the thudding freight.

CHICORY

1

"Alien"—still everywhere
by mid-July—those cool blue

stalkless flowers, deep as sky,
clench purple fists

by noon—low leaves,
like the dandelion's, now

the only life-trace
on their coarse sun-beaten

stems. Dawn's first rays
they're out again: taut corollas

spread like icy stars.

2

As I walk the weed-fringed
path to work, the early meadow

bright, I witness in this warm time
their brief lives—so delicate,

so rough—altered with each motion
of the light—squared stems

like the ancient 5-ridged
horsetail's, petals delicate

as silk. I walk
the meadow path to work,

breathe in, eyes glazed,
their scentless clouds

of blue. Heading home
late afternoon, there's not a sign

or trace (though everywhere
their sapphire abounds),

the sun's dull rays
now kindling a rough & weedy field.

MIDWEST FARM TRIPTYCH

Sweetcorn

Awake! the morning risible—
a shattering of low grey light
in badinage of neighbors picking "gold."
The rustled web of phalanxes
sifts earthblack air from sky.
Quaking sabers rise
to stab the sun.
     Seventh day—
the bedroom burrs alight with "shoat" & "crop,"
"weddins," barnyard ruse
of tractor-brats.
     Russet-swelled,
the sun breaks from the cornstalks. Larks
trill fenceposts, Angus crop through barbs—
wide orbs, like dull embers,
fixed on reapers as they chew.
     Near noon
banter trails. Dustclouds
rise from roads.
A combine drifts remotely toward an oatfield.
     Noon,
the stalks are still: faint hum
of sun on soil.
     This median of summer
(three weeks long)
makes confluence of sweet communal "gold."

Izzy Was Demonstrative

"Shit," he'd said,
when I'd yelled, "Hey, Iz,
you folks ever fix
that secondary corn?"

"Trouble with Americans,
they'd pine in a field
of plenty. Can't
eat around the bruise
in a goddamn peach!"

Swelter

The heat has filled the trees
& frizzled dandelion heads,
the cattle salivate & bunch
dank-furred inside the shed.
And everywhere the dung smell's
solid as a living thing,
& solid as another swarm the flies.
Drenched, we drudge the morning
patching screens, & still
the mad buzz & the midday darkening.
(The bigger take to pastureland
to clog the horses' eyes.)

Dead heat on the summer farm
has hatched a wild life-lust in the air,
that seems, at once, too thin.
All's gone to sweat!—
the smell of our own bodies, cramped
within these teeming walls,
has wound about us like a caul.

● ● ●

A horsefly,
slowly squeezing through warped frame,
falls to spin its death-buzz on the rug.

BARNMEN

Horizon's slow gold streaks
pitch morning light,

barns lift blackened hulls
on waves of corn.

Trucklights flicker,
wives trudge toward

coops, bend to cats
who leap their muddy

boots, the men's red taillights
fading on the hills,

the men who seek
Mae's Spoon, all muddy

warm—the coffee-scent
alive in minds

as gnarled hands wrap
cold wheels, rough-skinned & grey—

stained with morning
barnmud, "smelling pig"

as their wives quip, the wives
who trudge from coops

as their men fade
over the hills, feed bags

dragged like slack sails
by their sides. These men

stomp in the rattled door
&, playful, pound the counter—

"Fill 'er up," as Alice,
fat old Alice, grins

& sidles down the counter
filling cups. "Easy, boys."

Grimed fists pound the counter,
all in play. Rarely

do they talk, these men;
short, clipped "pig-talk"

when they do. All chafe
Alice, rarely glimpse

each other. All feel good—
stained overalls, worn shoes,

manure-ringed & holed,
among their kind. A few do chat

of pig-weight, crops,
the rain, but most stare

to the slow worlds
of their barns—watch

new-dropped squealers
bark & prance,

bite tails. Each in his barn,
the rank close air,

the huddled breathing mounds,
the grunts of recognition

when these men
homed back from coffee

clomp the hardwood ramps
to troughs, hose

into the tin, spattering
grey rivulets through straw.

They hump over the counter
there, these men,

pass a morning hour
with their kind. But watch

bemused, the looming walls,
the windy waiting doors,

knotholes knifing dust-rays
through the wailing

private galaxies of barns.

Pigeons

a memory

Sighting them—a pink grey fuzz,
a sense of their dark swollen warmth
below the rifled starglow
of a knothole in the loft,

watching them
through the crisp eye
of the .22 he'd taught
me moments earlier
how to aim,

riddling the beercan
to a hopping fiend
on the grassy edge of corn
gone tan and dry,
a skeletal rattling constant
in the leaves—

Sighting them, their throbbing weight,
heads wobbling like dull thought
into that moted blaze
of light,

the cross, fluorescent,
now etched stark
against one soft slow-pumping
breast—

the sense of a ripe offered fruit
or a babe's fuzzy head—

I jerked the trigger
to a thud and feathered
puff I'd known in some lost
dream, or what seemed
former life—
                              wakened
to the toppling
and the slap on the mud
floor.
            Now beside him—
leaning breathy on my shoulder—
but alone, I loved and hated
my young friend
who'd taught me his proud skill
with brother's trust,
                              whose father'd
offered us five bucks
to save the bales, to rid
the barn of pests.

SLEEPING BY THE RIVER, AFTER THIRTY

Dim instant's bat...Eyes
quiver open to slate shadow
as the Great Blue Heron
floats above, boned wings
outstretched—my prehistoric
dream?
      Glimpsed once before
in the bright noon, now centered
in the plum haze of my sunset-
softened eyes. My eyes
(time's lifting sense—dim form)
closed hours on this grassy
bank, above the risen river's
thick brown flow...

New thaw. Once more
the waking pulse
of early spring, a winding
river with an Indian name
I've known for years
as many things—play, loss
and distant memory—but now
returned and sleeping here
in waking dream, at last,
and wondering only
if the grey-blue bird—more grey
than blue, but somehow bluest
in the mind, bluer
than the sky itself
which always lucidly
deceives—will ever land,
boned wings gone soft, drawn in,
upon the scarlet branches
of my lids?

THE FEMALE CARDINAL

It's taken so many years
to learn this definite thing:
to know I love her dim-brown
plumage more than
a burning pride, more than
her fiery other's burst
through the spruce-row's
dark green shade. To know
those soft rose tips
of wing-feather & tail
hold meaning more
than preference or whim,
thrill more than the blood-leap
of her black-masked
shriller mate.
          An only jewel,
her coral beak's small glow
in snowlight livens
& alerts—his bandit's
shadow always swooping near,
his landing like a sudden
splash of blood.
          How many years
it's taken me to know
this thing, and know, this year,
that when a single morning glory
bloomed on the trellised wall
where last June's full vine
blazed—a single bloom
blue-circling its pearl
of yellow/white—and that was all—
I'd comforted my son & wife
with that's enough
to keep their presence here;
next year, weather constant,
there'll be more—but thought:
how perfect this *one* was,
a blue white-edged & faintly
pink, I'd seen—but never sensed
in its still form—before.

And now, cream throat
thrown back, her gentler
whistling, in short trills,
swells from the spruce's
coiling wave along the ground,
an endless yearning
trembling within.
              I barely spot
her rose beak's sheen
in twilight's needled grey,
her mate's shrill whistle,
faintly slurred, thin javelin of sound—
su-weet, su-weet, su-weet—
above, beneath, around
her isolated song, her soft *chur, chur,*
a rippling, a mantra raising morning light,
a single open flower.

SUN ON STEEL

As I walk the path
on certain sunwarmed days

that cleaves the red-flint mound
of the East-West Line

from glistening red leather
of the woodland

oaks, predictable in their
rustling drone, and solid

in late autumn, as the years,
again I feel the shudder

of the westbound freight
out of Chicago, predictable

in its hard pulse
as the sun's glint on wine

leaves—a murmuring through ground
feeling first frost,

a loosening of life
aroused, as thrashers, squirrels,

rabbits, crows begin
their free erratic dance,

all scurrying to nowhere
but just honoring

the energy of throbbing earth
and sound—a scurrying

their instincts never curb
or sense to tame, like ennui,

nor my eyes cease to
thrill to, as startled here,

each time, I watch the
woods take life, treading this path

that passes through the center
of sped life, and sun on steel.

CROSS-COUNTRY SKIER

Morning breaks, slashed rose,
across the long, dark-grey horizon.
Already in the nuzzling herd
(so close a single cloud of steam
blows up from mounds of winter fur)
the black bulls rise
on quivering haunches, rise
on braying heifers, keen to rut.

Sunrise: blot of soft, pearled light
forms bloodily its circle—scattered
hawthorns, ranging east,
hold frozen hills to sky
like black aortas...

Still. Slow pumping ceased.
Calves heavy, tingle warm.

I gaze from where my past tracks
end, those glowing rails
now filled with soft pink light...

     An old farmhouse, shred ragged-grey,
     slumps among the furrows
     of its cattle-weathered hill.

I feel their warmth, the chimney's
thread. Imagine their slow lives.
Warm and alone. Holding back,
as always here, I'm drawn...

         I turn
to pump again, then pause
to see the dark red light blaze down
my new-made tracks,
         the shadowed prints
of my dragged poles, beside the glowing rails,
like fossil-trails of horseshoe crabs—
an ancient race, or strange new
life—emerging to inhabit
a new land...

       Galena, Illinois

SNOWBLINDNESS

Only the red dogwood's
brilliant scar in the whitescape
down the river
leads me on. And still
the burning cold's
shrill light spreads through
me, as always mid-December
when the crust sets hard
as calcium, and throbbing bones
might keep a sane
man from his daily walk
along the river bank
in constant glare.

But let another man
partake his brittle glee
unmocked, his morning walk's insanity,
his thumping breast swelled
achingly within.

Snowblindness,
the deep sting of white brilliance,
the luster of an empty
mind, stunned seeing
in and out.

for my father

CROWS

20 below, our coldest
year, they huddle there
in the wasted field, swelled bosoms
flush—the delicate pulse
of torpid life—
claws snagged to the thrust elbow
of a dead elm's
ragged limb, wind
howling through its hollow
bole, they sway
in their fixed poise—alive—
the crows.
       They are the sculpture
for our season, of
our lives, claws fastened
to the coarse grey bark,
black forms on the grey sky
unmoved, alive.

DON'S MALLARDS

Breast-down ruffling
in the wind, the ice-floes
crowding hard
beneath the bridge—
soft rippling
we've been awaiting
winter-long, they swim
now in the loosened
tide as if the winter'd
never forged
the river hard, as if
Don never had to
tell me, black
weight of binoculars
slapping against his
chest, running up quick,
the wind whipping
his silver hair, "Dan,
they're here, they're here."

London Poems

*Whoever leads a solitary life and yet
now and then wants to attach himself
somewhere, whoever, according to
changes in the time of day, the
weather, the state of his business and
the like, suddenly wishes to see any
arm at all to which he might cling—he
will not be able to manage for long
without a window looking on to the
street. And if he is in the mood of not
desiring anything and only goes to his
window sill a tired man, with eyes
turning from his public to heaven and
back again, not wanting to look out
and having thrown his head up a little,
even then the horses below will draw
him down into their train of wagons
and tumult, and so at last into the
human harmony.*

—Franz Kafka,
    "The Street Window"

SKETCHING THE ASSYRIAN RELIEFS WITH MY WIFE AT THE BRITISH MUSEUM

Were it not mere alabaster, hewn
the better portion of 3,000
civilizing years, the Dying Lioness
of Nimrud, writhing in the grey
spew of an archer's flank-sprung
shaft, would continue,
year on year, to writhe
on the black friezes
of tossed sleep, to nudge
with her bruised snout
and dark closed eyes
into our dreams, like
painful words
that sputter eons to rekindle
in the corners of
the mind, like hunters'
fires verging
on our harmless seekers'
lives—stalking the
beautiful, found rarely,
never uncombined
with pain.

BAG-LADIES

(St. James's Park)

1

We float in some strange vision
of their making, our laughter,
careless, booms against their

skulls—grimed faces flinch, then
jeer where we drink tea
beside the pond.

2

All day they roam the park, up-
rooting glass, abandoned
news, clawing through

clogged trashcans for the
gobbets of stale food
and God knows what.

Or chuckle from the benches
at the passers, roses, ducks.
It's all the same

from those wood rafts that span
the edges of the pond
where we drink tea,

flurrying the feathers with
our crusts; it's all
the same—hilarious—

their leathern dust-grained
simpers haunt,
insist.

SOHO PROSTITUTE

1

Knee arced under lamplight
in the foggy evening drizzle
near the Olive Branch. Late,
the drinkers thinned...
                    Eyes go watchful,
craze—a gaunt mare's
stunned by lightning—
as two bobbies, aping
drunkards, stagger in...

2

Watchful...bobbies lounged
beneath STRIPTEASE
across the way—"Hey, love"—
a hiss. I turn.
"Hey, love, lookin'
for me?" She winks;
I scuttle on, stumbling
on a squashed quince
from the marketing
that day. Glance back,
she looks away, not quite
amused, tapping her toe.
                    Against the close
black wall of rain
I hasten on, summoning
those alley cats
of home, the echoed leers
of dream...Sottish,
grim, resigned...
                    But she,
knee lifted to the
light—"Hey, love, lookin'
for me?"—leans brazen,
wary, sly—still young, alert,
and qualified (and may survive)
till very old.

THE COPYISTS

They surround it...
Marking the air before their eyes
with whittling gestures
of their rules. Academy,
the final task, attachés
tight against their easels'
sides. We circle
silent, eyes turned in,
or looking past
await their wary
strokes. They near & pause,
step back again, with twisted brows,
some blocking in. Others, further,
lean upon their delicate
last strokes. *These*
we watch most...

The object's Rembrandt's *Adoration,*
magic light cast centuries
off Mary's downturned
face, the babe soft,
swaddled yet
in the warm glow...
The herdsmen, from the shadows,
watch transfixed—her
beauty in the lantern's
soft gold twilight
or the babe's? Perhaps
it's just the warm glow's
touched their hearts:
the drama—endless, always—
of the new light's birth
through dark...?

But though
some were quite facile,
others brilliant, or bold,
what made Rembrandt's shepherds
gaze—as mystified as we—
a mother's ripe face glow?

*—Royal Academy's Senior Class
at the National Gallery, 1981*

BIRD ISLAND, GREY LIGHT

We row again to the "bird island,"
wife sketching on the bank
above, obscured in the grey fog.

His small hand pink & white
with chill, gripped to the oar
that shudders downward

through the waste-chocked
foam, springs out in spray
with every awkward thrust.

But he must row there
with me—awkwardly against my pull—
so we founder like two pirates

from his stories, in the fog.
October's done. I'm thirty
in three days. Deep autumn gold

pools solidly beneath the island's
willowed edge. We enter
its mute bound—the golden mirror

shattered by our bow, we enter
grey & golden flickering near the shore.
The sluggish birds—coots, gulls,

the myriad ducks and geese—
are there. We rouse them
from their balled, neck-hidden

rest. There's sudden life
among the trees, and from patched
autumn grass, the lovely feathers

rise, a few go tense, the wary
leaping in. It's this he loves.
The rhythm of our rowing

and their sudden leaping in.
And even his dad's rowing, our slow
getting there again, has made him proud.

"The Bird Island," encroached upon
and left, the two of us
thump slowly back to tell

his mother how we roused
them from the fog, how we entered
autumn's willowed caves,

their secret gold,
where she sketches in the grey light
near the shore.

The Serpentine
Hyde Park, London

JAZZ MAN

(Regent's Park)

Immaculate. Hands a tan/brown
flutter like tossed sparrows
in the breeze, he stalks

the edge of where we sit
along the cinder orbit
of the rose-garden, each morning

more absorbed. Just conscious
of our watching
now, he leaps to one side

of the path, struts
stiff-legged, to the other,
spins, and bowing soft-eyed

doffs his glowing red
beret, his open mack
in early damp, still clean.

But how long since
he's snapped, how long
we wonder, till the mack

will stain with derelict's
smut, imaginary studio,
the humming crowd

a blur? We wonder
spellbound, although edgy
at his strutting blind

approach. But always
he backs off, bowing, aglow,
a blush of joy

beneath his brown close-shaven
jowl, at the seats' edge,
the concert stilled, shrill

howls and hot applause.
Mad? This perfect mime,
this great release for all of us

too sober to perform?

for Lydia

METAMORPHOSIS AND FUSION

Today I follow the woman
  with a beautiful
    horse's face—

brown beneath red sari, flapping
  in the wind. I follow her
    through parks, arcades...

run up...she's changed. A roan.
  Pommel and reins vibrant
    red, her mane—

coarse, dark—blown free.
  A horseguard leaps up
    (helm, red plume),

spurs her, rearing, into St. James's Park.

THE PERFECT LOVE

Perched on the pool edge,
aboard the QE2 (LATE SUMMER CRUISE),
a mongoloid idiot boy, stubble bluing
his slack jaw, rocks—humming—
    smiling up
    into his father's
    haggard face.
              Flat mask
calm, small irises soft brown
in the low sun. Blue suit
clasped to belly-white,
he rocks,
a tiny flutter constant
through his puffy lips
and dugs.
            Like a mirthful bodhisattva
he hums on, hums
his perfect love up to his father's
haggard face.

QE2: the British luxury liner *Queen Elizabeth II.*

Scenes from a Tragicomedy

BICYCLE

Like clockwork every spring
he's out again. Pumping up and down
by the trim lawns, neighbors

spraying, pruning, only vaguely
glancing round. This boy-man
washing dishes at the local

greasy spoon, keeping lawns
for veterans' clubs or links—
watchman at the town's

outskirt motel. His shadow clips
the hedges at exact times
every day. Lopheaded,

slick with brilliantine,
loose bangs dangling
in his mild eyes. License

never granted him, he slips
along the hedgerows
that surround our altered

lives. Grips clutched firm
in his large hands,
balloon tire chained tight

against park trees—or wired
to chill necks of main-walk
meters. Last job done,

he rests among old-timers
on the bench-green
by the tank from World War II.

On Sunday, flannel pressed,
black jack-boots shined,
he leans beneath the shade

of town-square elms,
half-seated, pedal up—
stolid and alert by turns—

watches us, old schoolmates,
our groomed children,
passing by. . .

PUMPKINS

They deceive us. And we them.
Carving our kids' whims
into their plump & gusty

flesh, handfuls of scooped seeds
mounding the newspaper-strewn
floor, bent to the scarred

oilcloth saved from the year
before, we huddle in the circle
of their scent—acrid & still—

blades tracing grins
already inked into their bland
& swollen skins that we might

alter, always, if we dare—
slight frenzy, grimace, calm—
by one swift slice or angle

of the wrist. Our kids, all goggle-eyed,
watch on. And on we carve,
refining lines—the razor's edge

of their gapped teeth—not quitting
where we might, now hardly
conscious that we carve

for them. . . . Finished now.
They stare, queer, droll,
triangle-eyed, crescent mouths

agape. Our kids squeal with delight.
Days beyond festivities,
the neighborhood grown calm again

in chill fall's leafless time,
they lean from the porch
ledge, dull orange, spent,

features caving in and turning
pulp. We watch them now
the most, and feel them kin.

Their smiles, as they rot,
become more real.

THE UTE INDIAN RETURNS

He'd come down, smirking, from the hills. We gave him work.
Odd, for sure, he spit at us and fixed the faucets wrong
in City Hall. Signed in an hour late smelling of rye.
But owing more, much more, we'd see it through. At lunch,
scalding our hands turning to COLD, we'd think of him, his logy eye,
and grin. Other jobs he botched. Finally, we'd keep him
from the plumbing, stores, our land. Mayor without vote. Amazed,
we watched the city sink back desert years to shrub, the mule
deer, goats, made gods. We planted grain, grubbing with our wives
in the parched earth. They bled, at night, from their soft knees
for weeks. Bruised, we rode Paiutes through the hills, clutching
bareback with our trembling thighs. He left as sudden as he'd come
one moonlit night in fall. No word. (There'd never been.)

We work long days. No effort to reform. No talk of change.
Most take to drink or puff the magic weed. Evenings we sit whittling
from the cool shade of worn stoops, feel sun's burning embers
prick the still mounds of our backs.

We died leaving our mystery enfossiled in the range.
He'd left us here one moonlit night in fall.

DOMESTIC

Palm Sunday. No new arrivals
here. My young son
burbles, gnaws his fist,
lobs up his breadfruit head.
The small hutch of his crib
beside my desk.
                    I watch the grey day
press the pane, the Wandering Jew
spill dark leaves, blood-laced,
from the planter's
lip.

He squalls awake, face
reddened like a tongue.
Slow gasps. I rise. He stops.
His presence here's
a gift of sorts, a sinner's
fast of mind.
                    And, no, I'll never
trim the Wandering Jew,
though she insist
it's time. I need its slow creep
down grey light.

There are moments when even the blind can see.

I Pry a Muddy Hardball...

1

I pry a muddy hardball from black vise
of gutter-grate—dried stiff: the turgid relic
of a frigid stormy month. Lopsided
in May's waterlog, seams split and coming
thin: ropegrit flecks the sawdust
in my hand. Fingers lock, an old machine,
hook down—pucker the coarse skin.
Lost spark, rumbling, creeps my forearms,
thighs....The years peel, puffy leather,
from those seams.

2

Bedroom dormer slightly lifted to the rush
of late-spring breeze, the neighborhood's
a windchime of miffed sparrows, ball!
and strike! "Yer out!"—shrill lifecommand
leaps through my fitful sleep. I shiver
wakeful near the warm hill
of my distant wife, want suddenly
to flee the heavy sleepsmell of my bed,
the things I am, am not. Want terribly
the deep wind of a toss or two, the clutch
of hammered glove, to ask if I might play
within their wicked, cheerful sorcery—forever.

MULBERRIES

The Italian Who Spoke

Where I lived
in the city of Milano
they are white as pearls
or dew. Not dark and red
like yours. And sometimes
when for hours we have eaten
in a circle
round the tree, we amble
down the valley, arm in arm,
to the swollen shore.

There is a season
in Milano when the ripeness
billows everywhere,
in the breasts
of the brown women,
in the white beads
of the mulberries,
when the rivers
flow together
and the mulberries
are full and white,
bows bending low.

And then in the faint
hum of afternoon, the amber
shimmer of the pulsing
sun, lips, fingers
glazed, we strip our clothes
and swim,
          trailing the clotted dust
of hauled cement, the work-mules
tethered to the willowed
brink, we swim.

Two or three of my townsfolk
drown each year
this way. They are too good.
Our bellies swell. They are too
good, *così, così,* it's true.

•

The American Who Listened

And having met pure strangers
by the Conoco pumps
on a sunny day in America,
hands purple-stained
beneath the sagging limbs
of a public tree, mouths
working sweet, we share
for moments, intimates,
this rich and terrible joke,
talking no more.
                    A sign,
it seems, that binds us
having met and talked
on a main walk
by the Conoco pumps
in America. Having met
and talked. A terrible joke.
Life risked in the honeyed
glut of joy.
                    Bound,
it seems, in a purple ring
on the hot cement
by the Conoco pumps
in America. On a sunny
day, forever drunk
with the life of it. And death.

•

The Tale Ascends

The swale. Their faces raised up
to the plumping boughs.
In a story told many lives ago,
it seems. . .

                    There is a river
in the city of Milano,
and by its side
they shimmer
in the white translucent
light

CROCUS GARDEN

When he'd come up, grinning,
accent thick, and asked
if I'd pitch in—a crocus garden
there in the parched
Utahn earth
outside our office door
(quaint vestige
of his English past?)—
I'd thought, *Look, man,*
at the mountains,
blue crags jagged
in the smoky heat, sunflowers
ablaze in fiery heights
of life and death.

But I'd given him my "dollah,"
wished him luck in his game quest
to order our sere
days, and watched dim eyes
go bright behind thick lenses
as he'd pocketed my gift.

There are the subtle fines
of being human.

INERTIA

Late night, the world iced still,
I try to read. The gaunt tom, with
a child's voice, again begins

to croak his shivered plea
into the blunt swell of subzero air,
pressed hard, like hollow lead,

against my window. I wince
against the thought of an inevitable carcass
latched to snow—black/white

shreds of fur branding for weeks
into the shadows of the backyard's wavy
crust. All's silent in dawn's ache

before first light. I dial Time & Temperature
so, when will and shame collude,
I might accurately write this to the world.

My inevitable missive of remorse.

TWO DOGS

Boston

My drunken neighbor keeps a dog
named Boston. Where he's from.

Scum feist. I murmured
if he rushed me one more time

I'd kick his teeth. Professor once,
his eyes teared crimson

in his trembling face. He told me
that he'd kill me

if I did. He knew my type.

I now walk far around
the dog named Boston.

The Collie

    gamy, matted, good as blind,
lumbers, weary,
    down the alleyway. Coughs once,
nose slumps to
    stained fluff of his chest. Squints
along the trail
    of weeds that brims the gravel's
crust. Now rocks
    his swelled frame back to straw,
snout poking through
    the arid blue that clots
with alley dust.
    This summer certainly his last,
a young replacement—
    Labrador, feet clumsy—on a chain.
Before he settles
    back to sleep among the dung and bees,
a foggy hum
    around his kennel's straw, he pauses,
as if questioning,
    croaks the hoarse shell of a bark,
signifying nothing.

PET SHOP

It started when I'd taken
my small boy, to pat the pups
& kittens—marveling for minutes,
then grown bored, wanting back
the sparrows and the squirrels
of his yard. Pets as much
and somehow more his own.

Now often I'm reflected there
alone, an insect in the red globe
of the white hare's furtive eye.
And then the neons' delicate
quick twists, in perfect ranks
(caught sudden in the corner of my sight),
will always pull me deeper

in, back to the dark recess
where the glowing tanks pulse up
their constant music of release,
a note that never seems
to turn or end. The bright fish-colors
blend & part, and blend again,
all sequence, dance. Their guts, even,

are beautiful, like seeds in pods
or embryos curled low into the half-
light of their taut translucent
flanks. But always when I've gazed
too long, the parrot, chained
to doorpost, fisted talon raised in spite,
calls me back in haunted

ribald glee, as if throwing
the humpbacked owner's voice.
Again, I must avoid his eyes—

from where he hunches by the feed-racks
on a stool. Almost a perch,
I cannot help but think.
And my thought snared, he watches me

& asks me how's my boy? A tiny sneer
that breaks two squints like fish-streaks
through his lenses' glinting
haze. He knows I'm never
there to buy, though I take
fishfood, birdfeed now & then,
the cheapest kind...

FISH-BOWL

Red/gold flash,
taut belly's steel—a lance;
above, soft-swelled,
the popeyed Black-Moor
weaves its silken
tail. "Louie and Ben,"
our infant lisps
and imitates their bubbled breath
a moment at his lunch.
But I stare hours past
our small boy's nap. All week
I linger by the bowl,
as if on some vague flight
through weed and dark—or lurk
the shifting hollows
of the sunlight's breathing
sands.

      At night
I nibble small green
leaves, eyes touching
the trembling watertop!

WHALES

Spouts lash the blue swell.
Slow humped crawl
through waves. All day
moving, jaws gaped
sieves—endless sucking chasms
of the small life
of the sea. Nights,
they brood low
depths, leeched flanks poised
bare inches
from the weedbeds'
furrowed sands.

They moor there
till the sun's pulse
when they rise, burst
the rutted surface
in brief domes; float
to warm chill
dorsals, follow ships—
gulls screaming, unwearied,
at the slow arc
of grey backs, plunge
for the stunned fish
their spread jaws miss. . .

But in rocked
sleep, between dim ports we seek,
their black throats
open wide. We clutch to ribs
and hover still—

breathless now
beneath their pounding
hearts.

HAWK EYE

for Neil Rettig, ornithologist

1

Months, the Redtail's mating: swoop
to deadoak limbs, a minute crook

of neck, stoop—*plunge,* a ferrous
coal, to rodent prey. Times,

his own eyes glow, quick coals,
glare down, in dream, upon their

rodent prey. Or hovers high, wings
flicking light & lashed to wind

against the azure sky. Of late
(scratched memos quip) he's not been

truly certain if he's watcher, watched
or mate. Or whether his own talons

have not scarred the rubble cliff,
small gusts ruffling the pearl tufts

of his breast. Or might he be (another
jest) the shrill hen brooding young: probing

urgent crops with morsels, dangling
scarlet, from her whittled beak?

2

Back home, the gathered months on footage,
reels: grass banks, forest borders,

mostly still. Slow days from the leaf-
blind, huddling small bones of her chick.

Mate, aloft, a spiralled distant speck.
Slow days from the leaf-blind, floating

grassland, mostly still.

•

. . .Late year, the sprouting hawklet
testing wings: the first low flight.

He stills the clattered beam
of the projector. Lights, applause,

we circle, smile praise. Attempt
to shrive the focus

of his distant feral eye.

Of Blight and Faith

BAZAAR

Meshed, Iran—1962

In the dim
stalls
of the rug hawkers,
the snake-eyes
of barter
leap
along the geometric
nap,
flower by
the lush *Kirman.*
Sheepskins
hang obscene
from other stalls:—
acid smell
of drying flesh.
Here
the taut jaws
clap,
but nothing's meant.

Nothing
but the blinding
of their children
weaving
black light
on cracked looms,
the belly-growl
for every *rial*
less.

MOVING SALE

How things fall away!
Where now? The emptied
room, walls yellowed
at the base. Milled
grime framing
where the carpet lay.
Where to now? a scorch
in faded wainscot
snags the eye. And they tramp
in, tramp in, rarely
a pause, as fingers sift
the faint nibble
of carp. Last things removed:
her linens, watchband, finally
my bike. The house thins
of the neighborhood. Stirless
moments. Sold. Welled
absence, chill, surrounds us
in the air.
              We pray
the frosts of memory—the buyers'
rapping on the door, diminished
in the melt of years—grow
much too thin to haunt.

TRAPPING CATS

Tomcat—back like a massy
coon—wailed spring nights
beneath the charred mimosa, split tusks
of living limbs. That wet spring
through, against the panes,
the blown leaves whipped and tapped.
Born on damp wind, rank urine's
pull, unwilled, had lured him
in—black, thick—to spur
the ring-tailed marmalade's
deft skulk of shingled roof:
green orbs riddling chimney-
shadows, weathering his shrill
demands.
            Safe within, the slow
dark come, she'd mince the russet
garden of our prayer rug's Tree-
of-Life, its nightingales and
geometric limbs: warm dyes,
as she settled, lapped the thrust
prow of her grin.
            Low sun, we set
the mackerel-snare, imagined its cocked
trapspring snapping down, the red
coal of his shriek piercing
the calm,—taut body beaten
senseless on the mesh, still
beating on...
            But now
unable to restrain, we inched
the blind again: black clouds, swelling,
massed the low night sky.
            Once more
the shrill stray's wail split dark, as slow
rain quickened, tapped its muting wash
over our sodden bait, that season's
broken limbs.

NOTE TO DOCTOR WILLIAMS AT CHRISTMAS

"To give a damn"
(and to not give a damn)—
most difficult resolution!

William Carlos Williams
when your Christmas greens went up in flame
by your own hand (town father's and life-giver's),
at once a conflagration and a prayer,
I breathed that thickened heat
with you. . . .
          Writing this on a bus,
your book in hand,
I thrill to faces beautified, this moment,
by the task of being human,

simmering, I imagine,
with the slow incessant flame
of gentle sorrow.

THE SCAVENGER

A man of loss conforms to loss...
He who conforms to loss
is gladly accepted by loss
       —Tao Te Ching

Sometimes at the late hour
a soft wind enters our yard's
gate,—something other
than the scuffle of the sharp-ribbed
stray, lank tail between bowed shins,

the bluster of chill gust
and limb, those raven crosses
on our winter sleep—
a weight of air, soft,
slightly moist and moving in,

now ticking as it works along
the study's wall, to where
the garbage waits, moon-glazed,
and oddly lovely in blanched disarray,
the garbage we no longer

try to close—a ticking
like the legs of a small insect
working on the paper's blank white
field—and then, once more,
her face, thin, weathered,

silver-fringed, in daylight
always gay, looms sharp against
my bronze-lit wall. I rise
to gaze through frozen glass
and barely spy the grey coat

scudding off like smoke, bulging
and yet always light—
the gate only a trace unclosed—
or one lone moonlit
cloud, dissolved.

A WINTER ALBUM

(manner of Chikuden,
Japanese scholar-painter)

1

All day the yellow maple leaves
scuttle down the windy streets
like claws, tap their fading lives
against the chill wood walls
at night. Another year.

2

Another year. Magpies light
on the snowy graves. Pinesap's
amber crystals limned
on trunks; sumac, faded orange
against snow. The magpies preen.

3

Today a girl I might
have known—black hair tossed,
faint smile sharp in the half light,
by the white graves beneath the pines—
walked by me in the snow.

4

The chill air bites. Taps bone.
Beneath the city hospital
the soft blue glow of ceiling screens
points warmly through the night,
fills snowy limbs, my breath. Warms bone.

5

Old men slumped on the glassy stoops
of liquidated shops. Abandonment.
Brown spouts clutched like ends of life
rise up through lamplit dark.
A listless calm. Like joy.

6

Old man bent to the water spout,
sagging coat trussed round him
with a rope, the girth
of one who'd eaten well
before he'd come to sleep nights
in the young tomb carver's shed,
curled behind brown wreaths,
the broken rock.

7

Magpie preening. Soft white down of upper wings
fluffed back, tail blown, a green flame
above the juniper's slow drip—a sloughing
of tubed sheaths into the earth's
first musk-logged scent, as graves
show names like life
emerging slowly through the thaw.

WINTER BOUND

There are scarred clapboards
that approach the winter
with glazed sides. And always
the covey of wino Utes
who rest against grey elms
on the rimy lawn
outside Skagg's drugstore chain.
And sometimes they move down
the lawn—a signal from the wind?—
crouch beneath the Bible Center's
placarded facade, dead eyes wide
to the traffic of this Salt Lake thoroughfare.
Hunker there but never go inside.

You near. They'll ask the time, then grinning
like dim brothers, cadge for change.
Of course, for the first meal
they've had for days.
You shrug and push them off
with you've no change. And, of course,
forgetting you, they try
again—breath foul, lisped tale the same—
as you pass back down
the icy walk, head lowered
to the wind—with pills
you've bought to numb the backache
of your pregnant wife.

At Winchell's

(all-night donut bar, Salt Lake City)

Glazed light: December's frost.
Beneath the Wasatch Mountain Range
the east glass wall blooms crisp
with ice-streaks, oranged
by an early sunburst
over slate-blue crests.

The cripple, wigged,
grotesquely squat, who's baked
the early batch, now sits
by his worn dame   ·
folding boxes—Winchell's boxes
with their gay-faced clowns
& donut garlands
festooning the letters. Intent,
he bites his lip,
folds each box with fixed attention,
loving it. She smokes
& squints at his thick hands,
still muzzy from her
night—watches them, unmoved.
Watches them press
fold on fold, with infinite care,
unmoved.
        He grins up quick
at customers
when the door bangs shut,
leaking cold & steam.
She shudders, scowls, put off.
He gazes from his boxes
to the mountains, brighter now
in their blue mists. Lifts
them all, with slow care,
to the counter—molds them tall
with final pats—
where a young girl, made up heavy,
halves the stack.

He sits back of a sudden,
takes his dull-eyed comrade's
hand. Her lour breaks
an instant's quivering smile
on her scarred & cream-caked
face, as the sun's bright column
prisms through the window.

Now. He strokes her sallow wrist,
her red-nailed hand
once more, & rises nudging boxes straight
that the young girl's knocked
askance. And limps back
to the grease-vats
for the glary noon's first batch.

QUAKE IN TURKEY
November 24, 1976

If the old grey-beard whose cramped black fist
shoved up between iced lips for days
could talk, he'd tell you

of the "deafening roar," of earth-dolls
piled down the buckled roads
of Muriyadye. He'd tell you

of his youngest, twins, pressed into the grainfield
mud, a pair of fossil-doves, where they had frisked
to image promised spring,

thrill of the deep Islam light
upon their summer chores, elders bowing east
for Mecca's grain; while everywhere

the pierce of muezzin's cry. . . . He'd tell you
how the tremors had still gnarled
two frigid days, survivors like stiff cattle

round the blaze. What left?
American supplies, the NATO tents, distant
telegrammed regret—It didn't matter.

They'd lost more forty years ago, frozen
for three days. Survivors once again
they will rebuild—and, summer come,

will harvest grain and bear their young
and, kneeling, bow to Mecca
for the sweet unleavened

bread, browning on the stones that covered sons.

FUGITIVES

(after Daumier)

Motion of flight:
human clotting
over coal-black hills;
stragglers, hunched as scruboak,
dot the crags. Frantic
they surge on, a solid howling
mass, red mouths
gaped from dun hoods
to the wind. Perhaps
they will consume
the ragged, limping mongrel,
clawing to the gristle
of his ribs,
a wild flap of cloaks
like crows' wings, rising shrilly
from the wind-thrashed
hills.
          On they surge,
hunched in the dark swarm
of endless flight,
          rage the barren reaches,
spurn a silent folding
with the cool and nameless
earth,

the coal-black hills.

GAMINOS

(Bogotá, Colombia)

clusters of them sleeping on the streets,
these homeless boys between the ages of eight
and sixteen   mostly runaways, they make for
the city where they form in packs—begging,
stealing, scavenging, living like wolves
                                    —UPI report

Streets

Black eyes
dart the avenues, quick flurry
of brown feet

time after time. They beat it
down the alleyways,
noon's prismed dust

scraped up in clouds
behind. Or separate
like chaff

to ride the shrill stream
of flocked stalls, converge
beyond

to prowl another street.
Low sun, they squat the littered
curb, silently part

spoils, munching pears.
The hawker's shrill abuse
cooled in the slow press

of lean jaws.

Sunday
(of Blight and Faith)

Dusk: they rise
on callused feet, slump back
through dimming fields

toward the church.
All crouch round
the mission priests, who dip

their sooted clothes
into a basin spewing foam
they clutch for, boys

again, in evening
breeze. Soup, bread,
the fathers bless them,

rise, and silent
leave the circle
of sly grins. Sharp teeth

gleam in afterlight,
the coarse black locks
made beasts'

by wind and rain.

Return

Morning, they crouch early
in the soft rose light
of business district

curbs, the rhythmic clop
of jades, the skirl
of new-washed

cars. Their eyes leap
from the flick of chrome—
the risen merchants' prize—

to slow wood spokes
of drays. Peasant vendors
prod the jades.

Fruit carts nudge home
to the curbs; a whinny,
as a whip cracks,

spurs their rise. "My wish?"
one told the priests, dropping
his eyes, "To be a merchant,

a man of responsibility."

MOTHER

Alone for years. Sons grown,
gone off. Ellis hazed,

an old Hasid
long since shoveled under.

She remembers whiskers, fine and white,
curled like tendrils,

yellow-tipped, down stiffened
blue lapels. The casket

of dark wood. Close faces, food-flushed,
watery eyes (the wafting swell

of gaiety and sorrow
intermixed)—and, yes,

regrettably, the cost:
a fine hotel, *tefilles*

deep-wailed, lugubrious—her savings
gone like that. But the old woman

no longer eyes the meats
she cannot buy

with jealousy. She's come to know
those streets she hobbles

down: the KROGER, JEWEL,
and NATIONAL, so vast and clean—

the promise they'd received!
The jeweled trays of fresh vegetables,

water-sprayed, in shimmering
rows, break joy in her rapt

and dolorous eyes—large, brown,
saintly now, past speech.

THE WARM HEAD OF OUR SON

This is the peace that
is possible in our lives.
—William Heyen

Today, the spring's first glaze
of warmth, headstones
glistening in the sun,

we walk among the names
of former lives—the Jewish,
under birches, lined along

the sagging fence, the Chinese
plot arranged beneath
the pines. But all is glistening

soft, the same, kindled
in deep rays of afternoon.
These days, a lull between

the things we do, that must
be done, we walk in
the slow time of early thaw:

soft ashes budding, junipers—
magpies pooled in pine-shadow
flick to sail up

sudden in their blue/green
trails of light. And now
we bend to smell the warm head

of our infant son, the stroller's
open top flapping in breeze.
It always smells the same

these days. Our breaths
inhale, exhale
like wakened bees.

City Cemetery, Salt Lake City, 1980

BIRTH-RITE

Feeding My Boy from a Water Bottle, Sunday Morning, Watching Trees

Catalpas fragrant. June.
Tubed flowers swaying, ivory,
against enormous leaves—

I lift the bottle
to his lips, that ruckle,
pouting, for his mother's
breast. We are alone.

Flowers twirling gently
from these bowed
and craggy limbs, slip
like fading comets
to the silent pool
of shadowed grass

below.

Glass

Close breaths purr
from steamed globes
parted by soft-flowered
screens. Small bodies
bound, alike,
to delicate glass worlds,
the hiss of mist.
Shrill chorus of wakers
rises, falls.

I watch his red hands
rise again
to clutch his croupy throat—
a flurry of small breaths
as mucus clears,
now rattles back,

each furious small breath
it rattles back...

My wife and I
stand by the cool, wet tent—
hands, limp, open,
dangled by our sides—
unable to move toward him
in this shrill
and delicate place, unable
to move from him
in this mute and terrible
love.

Spider

Today the sparrow, snared
by neighbors' housecats, tunneled out
by maggots, made you cry there
on the curb. I walked
on, angered, moments
without love. Remembering
just yesterday
I'd cursed our young boy
hard because he'd yanked
the spider down, web
tangled round those tiny palms
and, cooing, crushed it
hard. Crushed it, I now
know this well, with love.

Oh, how he whimpered
scuttling to his room.

NOCTURNE

for Theo

Voices rising from the trees...
 Those taut and brittle bows
  that brush against the wet chord
   of my small son's nasal sleep,

the breathing heard from here
 that means his mother's
  bedded down, that I'm below
   alone, holding this book—

scarf beneath my nightshirt,
 slight sweat tickling my chest,
  the heater low—its dark red cover
   closed and like a growth

from the chill bone of my
 clamped hand, and listening now
  to the far pine's sough and rustle
   that pulls in the glazed yard's bound,

the split elm's whistling scrape
 along the eaves, and—softer now,
  gone deep and still—the bushes'
   silvering gulf along the wall...

BRANCHES

They reach from icy drifts, these fallen limbs,
stripped in the blight-stiff willow's

creaking night. Black lines criss-crossed
gently in the snow—delicate

as tapestry, some fine & subtly
weaved design—but, then again,

the eye transforms to reaching arms,
thin knuckles splayed, saw drone

of the coming year, in memory,
renewed. The eye can toy

with this, and does: thin wisps
of calligraphy from some rare

sumi-e scroll, cross-hatchings
on Navajo pot or cloth, but now

most true, our seasonal of fear.
We look away, almost at once—

back to our plates, their rising
warmth. Separate & solid

in our soft malaise, gazing
at dead branches from this case

of glass & stone, from our perfect,
we hope timeless, shell of warmth.

THE CHIMNEY

(after Thoreau)

To build this. To build
this lonely way to heaven.
The white sand gathered,
grey rocks dug
from the shadowed littoral, the loon's
cry wavering like a hollow
face, my face
so long extinguished, in
the violent branch-crossed
red of evening
sun. I tow my dug-out
slowly through the chill
muck near the shore—
generations of small things
have trampled
or slow-sifted to this slime
my coarse toes knead.
To build this, I have given
half my life. It spires
not yet halfway up, a white-grey roughness
beckoning the falling sun,
the heaven's leaving
heat—like a last dull
finger of despair. Yet
I am not alone. The hut, firm,
rough-logged, now surrounds me
like a shell. Still, winter's nearing,
thin ice, here and there,
has slowed the water's
riffling pulse. But the screech-owl,
frozen sculpture in the trees,
will leap to truth—swift rising
in its secret heat—when
once again I near. It flies
away, dark pinions spread,
the rabbit leaping
from its hunched repose.

And the chimney, not yet finished,
purls its faint stream
from these hands. Gloom
of a cold season, once again
the wait for spring: the oozing mud—
bronze glitter from the railroad
bank, the slow grey spiral
lifework of a man.

BIOGRAPHY

Dan Stryk was born in London, England, where a number of these poems are set, but has spent most of his life in the American Midwest, which he considers his true home. He has frequently revisited London, most recently on an NEA poetry fellowship, and there conceived *The Artist and the Crow,* a continuous personal vision of American and British culture.

Stryk is the author of an earlier collection *To Make a Life* (Confluence Press, 1980). His poems have been anthologized and have appeared in numerous journals and periodicals, including *Poetry Northwest, TriQuarterly, The Missouri Review, Kansas Quarterly, Kayak, The Chariton Review, Commonweal,* and *Poetry Now.*

The poet has been the recipient of creative writing awards in both state and national competitions. He holds degrees from Southern and Northern Illinois universities and from the Creative Writing Program at the University of Utah, where he received the doctorate in 1981. Stryk teaches English at Northern Illinois University in DeKalb.

THE ARTIST AND THE CROW

Design by James McCammack
Illustration by Suzanne Stryk
Calligraphy by Janet Lorence
Photography by Lee Schreiner
Composition by Point West
of Carol Stream, Illinois,
in Century Old Style
Printing and binding by McNaughton and Gunn
of Ann Arbor, Michigan,
on Warren's Olde Style for the text
and Simpson's Gainsborough for the cover